Dancing
with the
Birds of Paradise

Dancing
with the
Birds of Paradise

❧

Karen Schulz

STICKY EARTH BOOKS

Some names and identifying details
have been changed to protect the privacy of individuals.

SE

STICKY EARTH BOOKS
StickyEarth.com

First Paperback Edition

ISBN 978-0-9986449-0-5

ACKNOWLEDGMENTS

My deepest gratitude to all who said I should publish when I was so uncertain.

To Arlene Butler, who read it first, to Melody Templeton who "put my feet to the fire" to get me moving on it, and to Annette Murray who beautifully illustrated, and lovingly guided this work into being.

To my family and friends who didn't know I had it in me!

And to Artemis, my cat, who gave up many a purr while I worked on this book.

Thank you —

I have written this poetry primarily for me — as a means for me to see how far I have come on my spiritual journey — but also for others who might find value in witnessing the wonderful joy and unfolding of a life that, like every other life, has also had its share of pain and challenges. The events that triggered my writing were encompassed in grief; and after I had written that all out, I found that I had more to say — in fact, I just could not stop! And that was exactly as it should be! Each time I write a poem, I learn something new about myself and about my world. As all of us live with pain and sorrow, all of us share in joy and beauty and wonderment. It is how I see it that I write here.

Poetry is "of the moment" and what I felt when I wrote each poem is not necessarily what I feel right now. But it could be. Some of my poetry is based more in reality than others, and it is for you to figure it out. I know the answers to that!

This has been a most healing experience for me, and my hope is there may be healing for you as well in whatever way my words speak to you.

Karen

TABLE OF CONTENTS

CALIFORNIA

HEART ATTACKED

So what is happening to me?
Perhaps I am having a heart attack, I thought. After all,
I'm at that age, that stage, where "things" happen.
And it has been going on a few months now, gradually
growing stronger and stronger — oft times taking my breath
away.
Nothing indicates a condition, however, but something
is happening.
It's certainly not unpleasant; it is more like an opening,
like my heart is expanding right through my chest out into —
Into what?
I noticed it first that afternoon when the story I was telling
suddenly ended. I was so stunned and shocked that I almost fell
off the chair, it took me so by surprise.
That little breathiness, that little opening inside that said,
whoa, girl, something's going on here!
And, indeed, there was . . . and I felt like an empty page, all blank and
      white
and glowy, like something needed to be entered on it . . . now!
Which is exactly what happened, of course!
Yes, my heart had been attacked — by all the many lies that told me
I deserved
no better.
And it stopped — for one brief moment, so that
it could change its beat. I felt it happen!
When it had readjusted to another rhythm, so had I.
The wonderful expansion is not only about what I can take in, but
      what I can now
give out. Do you get it??
I am writing a different story!!!
one of joy of excitement of loving of knowing — of experiencing the
      fullness
of Who I am!
And I'm well into Chapter One. It's so damned exciting —

I don't want to go to bed at night!
Can't wait to wake up in the morning!
To get on with it!
So someday, if you see an old lady dancing with the Birds of
    Paradise,
in the California mists or Mediterranean sunshine,
You'll know who it is
and what the next chapter is about!

ANOTHER BIRTH . . .

Perhaps it's like another birth, and I guess
we all have them at one time or another.
Mine came from death — a phone call saying Tom
had died, far away, in another land,
another world.
I still don't know
how,
or why,
it happened.
But I have my thoughts, I certainly do.
Heroin doesn't play favorites I don't believe
and it didn't now either.
He seemed proud to be clean — at least to me — but
again, he never told the truth to me, so
how would I know?
At best, then, he was playing a game he thought he might win
but in the end,
he lost.
Or perhaps he checked out, the life he was leading too
filled with too many complications/contradictions (I sure don't
know which)
and he couldn't keep them all straight. Was I one of them? Or do
I give myself too much credit for being
too important in his life?
I think so.
So after days of not being able to catch my breath,
I reevaluate it all.
I could call him a lying son-of-a-bitch and how could you do this
to me you creep you womanizer
(and yes, I was tested) you cheat — and I could say
far, far worse than that for sure.
But time no longer allows for that. So I stop the craziness
and I look
at the gifts.

He tried, he really did,
and had I been more open and honest — with HIM —
it all may have turned out differently.
(Note that I have to take some responsibility here also.)
But my body, now mine again, can find its way
back to its feelings — the ones he told me were
beyond my wildest dreams and I told him
were gone.
Oh no, he said. No, they're not. (Dare I believe him?)
He is right. And now I am free —
Free to love, really love. That which never was his to give,
Is now mine to claim.

FRIDAY NIGHT

Last Friday night I decided to build an altar
and I put on it all the things I had that reminded me of you,
which wasn't much for sure.
An old e-mail, the last letter I wrote to you, a cell phone
strap you forgot to take one time — and I forgot to return,
a picture of you against the brilliant Nevada sky when we drove
cross country — remember?
I suppose I could have added the sheepskin slippers but
I didn't!
I put them all on this beautiful cloth, and the picture behind it —
you know the one — which will be nameless here —
Oh, all right, the Orgasm picture!
And I lit three candles and incense and played this beautiful
       New Age CD.
But first I called your answering machine, still playing your voice.
       It said . . .
I will be back.
But you won't be — certainly not in the package you came in that
soooo appealed to me.
And I cried my last tears — almost — and said some prayers that
       maybe now
you are honest wherever you are, and that you are laughing and
       crying and opening
hearts among the stars.
We needed you here a while longer.
Why did you ask so much of me and tell me nothing?
Why did I sense your zipped soul around the lies you spoke?
When the time was right, I blew out the candles, and burned the
       e-mail and letter,
saving the ashes for
another day.
I stood up then, and put the altar away knowing full well
that I am better now.

THE ENVELOPE

I got dressed this morning
and, taking the envelope, I walk down
to the beach. It is cloudy and warm and there are only
a few of us, amidst the sand sweepers and the
gulls.
No whales or dolphins either.
I walk along and when I get to the pier
make an immediate right. Sand between my toes, I move
towards the pylons covered with barnacles, often a foot or more thick.
The tide is low and I walk out a ways. When a wave
laps at my feet, I open the envelope and out slip the ashes
of my last e-mail to you, the one you read but never answered.
Gone you are now, and the last remains I have of you are gone as well,
swirling amidst the pylons in little black patterns of death.
I believe you opted out, didn't you? You who demanded truth but
never gave it. And I, silly goose that I am, believed it was all my fault —
always. But my body knew something else, knew what my heart could
never admit, and slowly . . . ever so slowly, it is coming back to life.
And hopefully it is not too late.
I watch the last of the ashes swirl in the eddies and throw the envelope
in the trash, along with my old life.
And await the stirring of the new.

MARTY

A big man, intense.
Spent the earliest years abused
by his drugged-out dad.
So what did he do for 22 years
of his life?
The very same thing —
until he woke up,
and saw,
the next step was death.
So now he goes to Folsum
and helps others with
their rage and their pain and their
brokenness.
They may never see beyond the prison walls,
but for some, they'll get a glimpse
into an
opened heart.

We shared a friend, Marty and I,
who died looking for the very best
in a heroin fix.
It fixed *him* all right!
And as I cried my anguish out
in wretched pain and purple
anger,
he took me in his arms and
held me tight
until the tears were dried
by the gentle breeze.

Looking me in the eyes
and with the smile of the holiest
angel, he said,
Don't you know?
He just went Home.
He just went Home.

This man, who has seen it all,
has also seen
beyond the galaxies
to the very heart of truth.

And he touched, and healed, my soul.

OWEN — JULY

So I wasn't looking for someone that morning
and there you were. Certainly not my type
short and bald and I wanted tall with hair.
Well, anyway, we probably had driven three or ten miles
when it was obvious to me there was some kind of connection
But, hey, it was only a weekend.

I can't believe some of the things I told you about myself,
and in only a few hours you knew more about me than
my husband ever did in all those years of marriage.
Somehow it was okay to tell you my deepest thoughts . . .
I have wanted to do that for so long with
someone. And you were that someone.
It was so easy to tell you.
You didn't laugh or get angry or judge or anything like that.
You just said . . .
You're a human being, that's all. A human being.
But, hey, it was only a weekend.

It's hard not to get to know someone when the clothes are off.
And there we were, in a room full of no clothes and
it was all okay.
I don't think you realize what love you have, I thought to myself.
I felt so comfortable with you and everything you said led me
forward.
That Saturday night when we were together, and I shared with
you my darkest secrets,
You let me be . . . and do . . . I showed you how it was for me.
It was okay. I was okay.
But, hey, it was only a weekend.

It was more than that I found out.
I really liked you, loved you
and more than anything, wanted to share myself with you.
I didn't want to be wounded any longer,
but whole, and giving, and sharing of those
wondrous longings
so shameless and joyful.
This will not last forever, I know.
You have given more of me back to myself,
loving even those most tender parts,
and I thank you for that.
Time is not in our favor;
So I treasure every moment with you,
Every touch and caress
Each moment of slavery
To those one, two or three moments of bliss
and remember you.
Forever.

MOVING

You probably think I am standing back from you, he said. And
I have to admit I felt that.
It's just that it is so damned hard to think about your leaving
and I am trying so hard to protect myself.
Little does he know!! The thought of packing up and moving away
     from
this improbable little man who should **not** have entered my life
     — but did —
turns my soul into feather down and barbed wire, soft and prickly all
at the same time,
turns me into an arrow careening over those goddammed freeways
to pierce his heart wide open, where I might at last find
a resting place.
But . . . so far there is no resolution.
I can't recall anyone ever telling me they have to protect themselves
from me.
Usually I am the one who hurts, who goes inside where
that little girl sits, wide eyed and alone,
and I stay there.
But I am that little girl no longer, and now the hurt is
on the outside and I want to talk about it, to see where we
can go with this ache we both feel — if anywhere at all.
I e-mail him; he responds that he will think about it and somehow
I know he will, because that is how he is and that is why
I can love him.

HONESTY

I am really struggling with something.
You know, honesty is something that is very important
to me. Most of the time I am honest, but then again sometimes
I fail.
So okay I am not a perfect person.
But I need to tell you something, which I never, ever thought
I would do.
What I feel for you.
Maybe I don't know you
all that well, but I do know you deeply —
as you do me . . . for sure!!
I have this really hard time with you not being in my life —
or I in yours.
Somehow I want to be there with you always.
To hear you laugh,
to talk to you, to hear you say
There are no expectations.
I can just be me with you for whatever that is worth
and that is worth more than
gold.
I want to see you hold you kiss you caress your body with
soft oils as you do mine.
To sit, our bodies touching in all the right places, before
we . . .
move on to other things.
To lay my head against your shoulder
Knowing you will not
move away.
Could we drink coffee together or do laundry or clean house?
Together?
I don't know the answer to that question and there is too little time.
And that is why I have to
go away.

A DAY IN THE LIFE OF . . .

Let's see . . . what shall I write about today???
That I got a manicure and my eyelashes dyed . . .
Why on earth would you do that, you ask . . .
Well, like the hair on my head, my lashes too are
getting faded and should I ever need to use them in
a *flirtatious* way, (as if that will ever be a possibility again)
at least they will look like
Something!
At this stage, it gets
reaaaaalllllly tough . . .
Up in the morning (which is not as easy as it sounds)
after the coffee, and the bathroom scene,
it's time to start the day.
And this is where the work begins . . .
Wash the face, brush the teeth (or vice versa) and then . . .
Then it's a big splash of the toner (that's cool!), two different kinds of
moisturizer — each to maximize the other, followed by
the fade cream, the eye cream, and then the concealer designed to . . .
hide what the fade cream misses as well as those things that we are
supposed to
most revere — smile lines, laugh lines, crows feet, minimal lines,
maximal lines —
all those things that speak of wisdom and great knowledge
. . . (bullshit)
Age!!!
Now . . . on to the foundation which . . .
re-establishes that soft fluid, dewy the-envy-of-all-look
of youth . . .
On with the blush. . . the one that gives
all over color, and the one that paints the apples
of your cheeks. . . I am now good enough to eat!!!!
The eyes . . .
(Did I mention I dye my eyebrows too???
Now you know everything about me!)
So . . . the eyebrows at the moment look great!!
Ooooohhhhh . . . now it's the shadows, that will hold back, bring out,
make bigger, or smaller, doe-eyed or innocent, or vampish or assertive
— the eyes . . .

Got the picture??
Followed by the eye liner, at just the right spot — not in too far or
Out beyond — just to open them wide . . .
Mascara — that feminine enhancer which almost every woman vows
that she cannot do without on a dessert island . . .
glides over those newly dyed eyelashes, lengthening, strengthening
opening, revealing
those contact lensed windows to the soul . . .

We come at last to . . .

The lips.
How do I do them??? Let me count the ways . . .
First I plump them, moisturize them, line them, fill them, color them
any or all the shades of the spectrum of color God
ever thought of — and then some! Followed by
a hint, a tint of gloss, which adds that lickable, kissable
wet bit of shine . . .
Oh, men, I sense your desiring, your deep, deep breathing . . .

I CAN NOW BE SEEN IN PUBLIC!!!

And do you realize I did not even mention the shower or hair?

So now that it is four in the afternoon and I am ready
to walk out the front door, I have an hour
to do the shopping and fix the dinner before I have to reverse this
whole routine again — probably around seven-thirty or so.
Tell me, what man would put up with this??? . . .
If I can find the time, I think I will curl up with
the cat!!!

EARLY MORNING

The sun is out this morning — June gloom has
                                    no chance today! The rising promise of
                    heat radiates off the
flashing waves and fresh mowed sand.
            Noses peak from foaming waters . . . seals
flip out, seeking their audience and, finding few this early
                                    who appreciate their antics,
move on.
The fishermen — or should I say *fisherpeople* — although
                    they are all men as far as I can tell —
cast their lines, sleek shiny minnows flying out over waters
teasing the Big Ones
                                                to the hook.
I wore long sleeves to keep off
            the morning chill, but that wasn't necessary — the sun
caresses me everywhere like a lover who
                    knows my desperate need.
                            This little dog, wearing a Pucci-like scarf and
            sun visor — no less, wiggles up to me as if to say —
Aren't I the most beautiful thing you have ever seen?
                    And, at that moment in time, I say Yes!
And off we go again.
                            The beach is wonderful, isn't it?

THE COMPLIMENT

You know, I think a lot about
love. And I wonder when it happened that I began to feel
there was not enough . . . that I had to hoard it — like wheat during
a famine and water during
a drought.
Take it out and look at it, turning it over and over
again, checking to see if it was real or
just pretend and then
putting it away — hiding it.
I still have trouble trusting it — and those who say
they love me.
It has almost caused me to wither up
and die so many times during my life.
To this day, for me to acknowledge and say
beautiful to another, particularly regarding looks —
(my ego says that you have to watch out for the
pretty ones) — or to recognize another's gifts, I feel so left
behind. And to acknowledge other's worthiness
only diminishes mine.
So as I step out in the fullness of
me, I am ready to let go of this
nonsense.
I have a lot to learn about giving and
receiving for sure, but today, I make a promise to
practice both . . . to give
compliments that are truly heartfelt. For it is
in giving that we receive, so it is said.
And this time when I turn love over and over
I will see you — and me — in the golden
reflection of my heart.
I will smile and know that
I am just fine, and have been,
all along.

TRUTH and CONSEQUENCES . . .

I didn't exactly lie,
but I didn't tell the truth either.
Like how do you tell someone that it can be
just wonderful either way, particularly when
that is the truth!
When it didn't work together, I tried it
myself in the hopes that we would
both be satisfied. You wanted it as badly for me
as I wanted it for myself,
the joy, the pleasure of both of us participating in
that special sweetness.
But reality doesn't always meet expectation, or vice versa.
So to end the agony, I said okay to what was
not the truth. Does that mean I am not true to myself, to him,
to God . . . or what??
Is that Okay?

BOTTLE BRUSH AND HUMMINGBIRDS

Bottle brush trees paint the air with brilliant tips
dipped in red against the sky.
They stroke all different shades —
    fiery and fierce
    soft and caressing.
Tiny green wings beat furiously
to get their share of sweetness red
and then stop — to take their leisure and chat a bit.
And off again they go.
Picasso could do no better!

THE LADY IN RED AND THE SNOW QUEEN

I know **you** all know about it — about the
Lady in Red aka Rich Lady — and the Snow Queen. Well,
I sure didn't, but I sure do now!
Never did I think I could one hundred percent fall in love with
        one of them, much less
Both of Them, but given my state of mind recently, when I first saw her
        (the Lady in Red),
the warm, sweet blush of her skin, the way the sun seemed to just
        radiate right off of it,
I knew — just knew I had to have her as soon as I could.
But then I saw the Snow Queen
        (these names — don't they just get to you)?
She was soft and pink as well, but it was her white flesh that just sent
        shivers up my spine.
How would she taste against my lips? Juicy and wet?
Yes, yes, yes —
I could already tell that!
But then I pondered — What would it be like to have both?
And the gods asked, in their infinite wisdom, have you ever done this
        before?
And I, blushingly responded, well, no not exactly,
but I think I am ready — I think
It. Is. Time.
Oh, such sublime passion, such incredible pleasure!!
The sweetness and juiciness was beyond anything I could ever have
imagined, dribbling their tastiness all over my body.
Now sated and filled, I cleaned up a bit, and caught my breath.
I looked at my hands that had just caressed this lusciousness
And I count the days hours minutes until I can once again
        hold them
when the nine am bell rings . . . and
the Peach and Nectarine Stands at the Farmer's Market open for
        business!

SCHLEPPING

Today I went to a sporting store to buy
a few things (like, any woman can just buy
a few things)
for the rafting trip next weekend.
A man was there — also shopping for
a few things (and men *can* do that)!
The clerk told him where he could
buy something unavailable there (nice, eh?)
but he would have to schlep a good distance
away to do that . . .
So, laughing, I made some comments on schlepping as well,
then schlepped myself up to the second floor for
my "few" things.
Soon schlepping up the stairs came the man, Len his name,
to suggest that perhaps we might have gone to school
together — and have you any idea how long ago that would
have been?
Realizing that he could not have known me from
way back then,
I recognized a come-on right there in the Big Five —
which is not too bad a thing for an aging rafter wannabe . . .
We spent some time chatting and can you imagine?
We will be schlepping out to dinner
Thursday night!

ZIP!

Zip! Did you see that day
go by?
I hardly saw it come —
or go — it seems.
The sun, rising at 5:11,
fast forwards so fast my
head gets dizzy
trying to catch a glimpse
of it before, hurtling
towards the ocean floor,
it cools and refreshes itself
once more —
rising again to
a world that barely notices
its brilliance.
Radiantly it reveals itself,
shining its healing rays
into the dark gloom of our lives.
If only, if only
we would choose to let it in to
those very darkest corners,
we could see
our own brightness,
dusty with shame and covered
with guilt
waiting — just waiting for us to
embrace our own sunlight
which stays —
and heals us — forever.

FISHIN'

As I walked to yoga class
this morning,
an old man raised his hand as if to
high-five me.
A no-bath-for-five-weeks fragrance
Wafted 'round him.
Goin' fishin' wif my sister! he grinned at me
with a half-toothed grin, eyes looking into a different
world than I was looking at, for sure.
Goin' fishin' wif my sister! And he began to dance.
Have a great time! I said, and smiled back.
For who am I to say
it's not the truth.

WHITE

The white rose petal softly and gently
this way and that,
twists and turns and flutters
until it reaches grass,
and then, with the breeze,
flits just a bit more
before settling down.
The white butterfly softly and gently
this way and that,
twists and turns and flutters
until it reaches grass,
and then, with the breeze,
flits just a bit more
before settling down.
How do I know the difference?
I don't.

WORDS

Today is the first day I felt
I had no poetry to speak. It's only been
two weeks since I started writing here and
words have been tumbling out like the wind-driven raindrops
in a storm that follows hot and humid days,
sent to cool my fevered soul.
How wonderful it is, then, to see one's feelings
OUT and clear, to touch the words and know they
will not hurt.
Washed and cleansed, they are now just that —
words — from that deepest part of me, my soul,
now fresh and renewed,
at least for a while.
And as I look at them, I see that all along
they were crystal and pure, speaking only
of that part inside still struggling —
still on its journey.
So I fear no longer and tossing the words high
into the sky,
I watch them transform into
twinkling stars.

SUBLUXATED

So . . . I am in this big rubber raft,
along with six others on possibly
the most beautiful river that just
takes your breath away, no doubt!
And we get stuck on this huge boulder,
or so it seemed to me, but perhaps it really was
just an ordinary one that got in the way that most
perfect July day.
And newbie that I am, over and out
I went,
ass over teakettle down those swirling percolating
crystal brilliant shimmering waters,
backwards no less!
Bumping crashing rolling tossing
this way and that
missing and hitting
other boulders, one after another —
(and **these** were the big ones!)
all sides, up and down, until
a few hundred yards further along
I was hauled in,
proud of my survival and feeling no pain — then.
Later, checking the assorted colors
of even more assorted parts of
my body, all quite beautiful I might add — the
colors that is — I notice one of my fingernails
gone — not there! And my middle finger
not looking like any middle finger I have
seen before!
The boulder did it! It hit straight on my finger!
What next folks? I did this a lot as a kid, fingers
straight out as I ran to catch a ball.
Jock I was not!
And not now either. The second doc I see
finally figures out it is subluxated — two bones no longer
meeting each other, I think.

Splint, tape, little movement, time ... surgery — perhaps ...
What, may I ask, does this mean in the scheme of things?
Only that I took risk, and like every risk, I
might just have to go though a little — and maybe a lot – of pain
to see the beauty in a world
never, ever before
known to me.
I am, indeed, most richly blessed.

MARY ANN

This morning I checked off another week
and realized
there is not much time left here.
I started checking off time
a year ago June —
don't ask me why. I guess
I was feeling homesick and it helped me
focus on — yes — I could go home,
but it would be at least 67 weeks.
Mary Ann did the same thing, I think, and
once she got home,
she *went* Home — all the way — because the
cancer got her shortly after
she arrived at the house she loved so dearly.
It was so quick that she had no time
at all
to do the things she wanted to do
when she retired —
reconnect with her small and loving family,
fix up the old house,
walk the parks she knew so well,
and once again, play in a
Minnesota snowstorm!
I went to help her out during the
few months she had left,
and watched her disappear
as the cancer ate her up and the
cigarettes she loved so much became
the smoky shroud that enclosed
her tiny body before
the coffin did.
I think about that now as I
pack up the boxes
of my life that will go
on the van cross country to
home.

But it is time, and no matter
which home I will Live in
for now,
I will embrace the opportunity
to live whatever life is left
with grace and joy and gratitude
and memories of
a most incredible journey.

THE DREAM

I had a dream last night.

Lying on the bed,
you were rubbing my back,
and I was feeling my body —
and spirit — radiating
with your touch.
Gentle and strong,
you were moving
into all the very right places,
and the love you were
giving me sent strong volts
of energy to
the very tips of
everything.
I must tell you something, I said, something
very difficult for me to share with you.
I have made this promise to tell you
the truth of myself,
and you said you would
hear it.
I felt your touch stop, and the energy trickle
slowly down into a dried puddle inside of me.
When I turned over, you were
gone,
and I was alone.
I never even heard you leave.
Whose fear was it — yours —or mine —
that spirited you away from
my heart?
Or were you
ever there at all?

THE LOVER

I have just finished a letter to
an old friend. We were lovers
once upon a time when we were
far younger than we are
now.
He is moving away to where it is
quiet, peaceful and life is calm.
Now, he waits for only one thing.
How I will miss him; lovers no more,
we are still the best of friends who
share the fun of having spent hours in
the deepest forests eating sandwiches and drinking
sodas, before slipping under the leaves,
and dissolving into hours of discovering
all there was to know about each other.
It was before West Nile, and Lyme and unclothed,
we never thought of anything but
soft luscious breezes — and hands —
and lips everywhere.
He wrote poetry to me — gone now because
it dared not be saved.
But I remember the surge of pleasure each line
held as I read them,
opening me up to what was yet to come!
How wonderful that time was!
But I am making new memories now.
That is the gift I have promised myself
in this newest chapter of my life.
The way it is to be.

THE CHIROPRACTOR
   (with thanks to Arlene Butler)

I visited the chiropractor the other day
to get a few things
checked out.
Nothing serious, said he, except that
your head is like 2 degrees off center —
well out of alignment from where it should be.
And . . . blah, blah, blah, blah,
he said, then
told me what I needed to do
about it.
When did I start
leading with my head? When did it
start moving out before my body did —
which is exactly what it does, as I
see myself reflected in
the mirror.
Hmmm, how interesting. Perhaps my head
went forward when my heart shut down,
when I knew that something had to be in the lead,
to get me to where I needed
to go, and the heart had so lost its way.
For all these years, my head moved out there,
filled with wonderful ideas, meaningful strategies,
moments of brilliance, taking me into
all kinds of different territories,
where kudos for intelligence were heaped
on me — and kept me in check.
But when I took another look at my life,
I saw that all the love my heart could give
lay crunched under stooped shoulders
curved around to protect it from all the
hurt, my head having been the lead-in
to my life.

I was surprised the heart was still thumping.
As the chiropractor straightened me out, I
felt it once again pounding proudly
as if to say, Here I am and I have so much to give —
thank you for at long last noticing me!!!
So with shoulders back, boobs out, back straighter,
I am moving everything into alignment —
as I am meant to be.
And my little heart, growing bigger with each beat,
is keeping time to every song I choose
to sing.

THE MARRIAGE

It lasted thirty years.
Enough time to grow old together,
if that was to be.
Golden years, so much of it,
filled with the love of children
now grown into beautiful and loving men.
Time for a man to become successful,
to show the world how talented he
really was. And he really was.
Parties, travels, enough of enough —
How much better need it be?
Somewhere along the line, I lost the line.
Whatever joy there was — for me — was
washed down the drain with soapy waters,
rinsed with tears.
So I grabbed my courage and said goodbye,
to all that was easy and all that I knew.
It was a new chance for him as well
to find the love I could not give —
then.
Three weeks later, he found her. And now has
all that he ever dreamed about — a woman of
class, monied, a house at the shore, her home and his,
travel, and time to enjoy.
And I?
I have found myself —
a very new young-old woman,
bursting with joy and a heart filled with love
eager to open.
Today I was asked, Why are you so happy?
For that, there is no answer.
I just am.

PASSION

For many years I lived without
passion in my life —
or so I tried to tell myself.
Why in heaven's name would anyone do that?
That's the question I was trying to answer,
the question that came to me as I was trying
to save my favorite geranium plant from
being eaten up by big green wiggly things
that wanted to consume my most beautiful flower.
Right then and there I knew the passion I felt for that
brilliantly colored plant. To save it
from that which would
kill it, I had to take
immediate action.
And then I got the connection.
There have been big green wiggly things in
my life also, but I would not let
myself look beneath my carefully tended
leaves, because outwardly they looked
just fine.
When they began to tum yellow and brown,
and when little black dots of you-know-what
littered them and those beautiful leaves
began to shrivel and fall,
I had a choice to make
right then and there.
Could I let this beautiful flower wither and die?
Or would I have to clean up my act so that
the beauty of who I am — the passion of my
flower — be allowed to bloom
before it was too late.

I decided to try the cleansing process,
to allow a loving hand to come in
and pick out those big green wiggly things
that were sucking me dry, changing my colors,
eating away at the very most
beautiful parts of me,
so that I might live again.
When that was done,
when I was all cleaned up,
my leaves turned the most
vibrant green, inside and out,
and the flower I never thought
would make it
grew wildly and passionately, deep and richly
red.
The gift of myself — in all ways —
can now be seen
by those who wish to
touch and love its brilliance.

OPTIONS

I don't think I am going to write anything today.

Why not?

Everybody needs to take a break from their own
change and
personal transformation, right?
A chance to sit back and smell the roses, put the
feet up and watch a little tv.

Smell the roses, eh? Like that incredible bouquet
sent to you this week?

God, aren't they just the best? Their fragrance and
the glorious colors so unlike any roses I have ever seen
before — What a gift these are to me!

Indeed. The total perfection of buds
ripe with potential fully
opened today, showing their
magnificent radiance—just for you.

You got that right, honey!

And tomorrow, just as you have
begun to fully appreciate that incredible
beauty,
a petal will fall, and then another,
and then another . . . and then
another.

Okay, so what are you trying
to tell me?

I am telling you that change
and transformation are like the petals —
they will fall away, wither up
and soon die, if you sit back
and ignore
what you at long last
see —
your own fragrance and fullness and ripeness.

To sit back is not an option?

Did you not do that for most of your life,
intrigued by the drama, the
comedy, the life stories of others,
while fully choosing to sit back
and never live your own?
Is that an option for you
now?

You're right. There is so little time.

You're right. There is so little time.

GETTING IT

I think I am finally beginning to get it.
That I am okay, really okay,
just as I am.
Why has it taken me this long to get
to this place?
For so long I have based
my Self on a picture that really
wasn't me — or was it?
Well, never mind, it isn't all
that important any longer.
I think particularly about
my body now.
You know, it really isn't half bad looking
as I peer at myself in the mirror —
a little loose in the flesh, a bit
paunchy in the tummy, and a pretty
sizable bum,
but the boobs are still perky — not like
a 20 year old — but
up there pretty good.
Now I am having to retrain my body
to reconnect with openness,
with no restraints and no fears,
unlike in the old days, when passion and loving
were all done
in secret.
Secret feelings, secret lovers,
secrets separating myself from
my husband
because I could not give him
what he wanted, because
it was not
what I wanted.
And there was no openness,
Ever.

At this stage, it is not
an easy transition and
if I did not have a lover now
who allows me to be
Who I Am and says
It's okay, Karen, you are absolutely
okay,
I would be pretty
undone about myself.
For me, that is what
opening up now is all about.
And it is such fun trying!

A DIOS

In the crossword puzzle today
was the clue, "Mexican sendoff" —
 which, of course, is
Adios.
I look at the word and say it several times
to myself,
Adios, Adios.
Such a beautiful word, so rich with meaning —
Adios. A Dios.
To God. Go with God.
We say 'bye, see ya, so long, or maybe even
Take care, but how beautiful to say
A Dios.
How wonderful to send someone away with
such words, with such love,
with such confidence in the comfort
and caring of God.
How rich are we when it is
said to us!
I cannot change the way
we say good-bye in this culture
but always, always
I can send a blessing.
Adios. A Dios.

EXPANSION — OR CONTRACTION?

It's about expansion or contraction, isn't it, Karen?
Arlene and I were talking today,
Arlene being my therapist,
Because if you are wanting
to contract when you move back
east, perhaps we need to schedule a few more sessions.
And at $100+ a pop, I started giving what she said
considerable thought.
She is right — a student no longer,
it is now time for me to become
the teacher — uncomfortable as that may be.
I don't know enough, I thought. But that
has been my MO forever. It has kept
me waiting for a Report Card to tell me
I have passed, that I am okay.
I have graduated now, and I have enough
diplomas to hang on my wall.
I am strong enough to share my light and
give of my gifts.
I am capable enough to learn to parallel park
and not get lost reading a road map.
I am brave enough to open my arms to
my gorgeous granddaughter and to her wiggly,
squirmy baby brother.
I am willing now to open my heart and let
everything inside out,
because an opened heart is the most valuable
thing I have to give.
I **have** grown up and I dare to live my dream,
if not perfectly, the very best I can.
I can do nothing more than that,
That is now who I am, and that is the choice
I choose to make.

E-MAIL

I get all of these wonderful e-mails
telling me the state of the
world, how much longer we have
until it's All Over for
All of Us,
how to access sexually explicit
material,
who should be the next President and
why and . . .
And . . . ta-dah . . . How to be Saved.
Now, that is where we get to the tough stuff.
I haven't the foggiest idea what it means
To be Saved.
I never thought I wasn't and if I did need
To be Saved,
what from?
I grew up in the Age of Guilt, and
got a double A plus in this subject for
most of the years of my life.
Rumi says there are hundreds of ways to
kiss the ground and I say there are just as
many ways to live a life of fear, anxiety and
yes, guilt because I didn't kiss the ground
just right.
But lately I have discovered that my guilt
was the reason, or perhaps, excuse, for me
not being fully ME, and somehow I don't
think God meant it to be
that way.
In the time I am living now, my sense of
God has pleasantly changed, and I
think He is getting a big chuckle out
of that.
We are co-creators, He and I, and
it is my joy and my honor to do
what I can to bring our love to the world.

No shame, no guilt, no fear, no
doubt,
Just He and I working together until my
job is done, and then will I be cradled in
the Arms of Love until
the next assignment.
Pretty exceptional way to live this life,
I say!

HEADLINER

I was asked to do something quite wonderful
the other day — essentially to be
a headliner . . . because of all the knowledge
I am supposed to have.
Now I have always chosen to be a sideliner,
sitting beside a headliner, maybe,
but always being the one
who assists — and not leads.
So as I thought about being a headliner,
no longer a side liner,
I offered a one liner . . .
And I said "yes".

THE POOL

Last night I swam in a garden's pool
shimmering with the colors of
deepening dusk, of glowing lanterns
and flickering candles,
and the distant lights
of a distant city —
listening to the music
of a Mystic Journey.
The sweet, soaring sounds of flute praised the night
and floated on waves of fragrant space,
over soundless ripples of mirrored glass.
Silently we listened to the rise and fall of the music
of a soul, gently raising the sounds
of traditions far away and seldom heard.
Silently we listened, as the notes themselves
caressed our unclothed bodies
floating effortlessly in the gentleness
of suspended time.
Silently my soul opened to the magical
rhythms so unlike its own.
As the melodies flowed through the thirsty
chambers of my heart,
I felt again the amazing grace
of an amazing God,
Who opens me up to receive
such amazing gifts.

THE CHOICE

When will the pain end? my friend asked me,
tears streaming down her lovely cheeks,
reflecting on a relationship which should
have ended a long time ago,
but did not.
I watched her watching me, knowing that there is
no answer to this question that she could
accept — now.
How many years I lived with a similar pain,
outwardly looking for that special
something
that would dry my tears and make me
happy again.
It happened when I least
expected it and only,
only when I made the choice to
see my world differently.
For the first time I realized I had
the choice — to live in misery — or
to live in joy, and the choice
was totally and completely mine.
To come out from all the
unnecessary pain in my life was what
I needed to do.
And there was still quite a lot of
necessary pain to deal with
first.
The work is not easy, but when one
sees what the ultimate outcome
will be,
there is just no standing back.
Run — don't walk — to that nearest EXIT
was exactly what I did.

How I would love to take my friend's hand and
walk her through the EXIT of her old life
into the new.
But that is her choice
and all I can do is to be there –
waiting.

DISCUSSIONS

I love those philosophical discussions about . . .
If I had it to do over again, would I? —
our lives, that is.
And to almost a person,
on the very deepest level,
no one would do it any
differently.
The same choices.
The same decisions.
The same outcomes.
The same joys and woes.
So if that is indeed
the case,
why do we act as if life is
such a drag
instead of such an
incredible Adventure?

MULTIPLE PERSONALITIES

I felt like I was four persons today.
I don't know — perhaps it was the slant of the sun
that brought up all the different feelings
of who I am/was throughout the now many
decades of my life.
I remember the four year old, tousled hair
and opened arms, who got on the streetcar and
sang her little heart out —I'm a Little Sunbeam —
to the delight of the riders and even more
to the absolute delight of herself
on that lovely golden sunny
August afternoon.
I remember the teenager, pimply-faced and pudgy,
wondering who she could become in a frightening world
of adolescent hormones raging against her self-control
and fearful of moving out into a world she did not understand.
Who silently, silently wept alone on golden
late August evenings.
I remember the mother, tired and lonely, putting her own
tousled hair children to bed and sitting on the patio, dreaming
dreams of life moving past, as the cicadas and crickets
sang their songs in the heat of
late August evenings.
And she could not join in.
I remember the moment that said life could be more
and I must search it out
that August day those years ago.
And now the little girl sings again, the hormones are no longer
the issue, the mother now looks *up* to those children to
plant kisses on their whiskered cheeks
and the tousled haired woman now knows
that it was all just as
it should be.

AUGUST 11th - AUGUST 18th

I arrived in rain
and leave in fog
and there was little sunlight
in between.
A darkness here
no doubt about it.
A heaviness — as if
the stagnant air
bares down on bodies
and souls
too burdened to lift it off.
Who am I to think
I can make a difference?
Who am I to think
I can't?
Soon the cat and I will leave the California sunshine
and move back
to where it all began.
The light will change, but what I must
remember is
the Light will be the same.

SAYING GOODBYE

WEEKEND

I was with my son this weekend —
now a man, strong and bright,
with a twinkle in his eye and
such laughter in his soul!
We worked well together, he and I,
— me supervising
— he doing
all that needed to be done to
ready the house
for my return.
We went to Home Depot,
of course,
and when we were finished,
we drove back in time
to the land of his childhood, a few miles
away.
The old house looks good,
although the willow tree is gone,
and ugly red draperies cover windows
where once
only sunshine looked in.
He said, "Mom, this is really tough,"
I said, "What do you mean?"
"I want to go in that door
and sit down in front of
the big old TV like we did
for all those years.
I want it to be
like it used to be."
Don't we all
at one time or another.
Life is funny that way and
while we yearn to move forward,
we also yearn to move backward —
to once again just sit in front
of that big old TV.

But what opened my heart most
was the fact he had
such happy memories.
And I told him so.
"Oh, yes, Mom," he said. "So many happy memories!"
What more could a mother ask for?
I did my job and
I did it well.
We started the car again
and drove back
into the present.

WHITE PENNY LOAFERS

On the flight to LA
I sat across from an old
woman, gray-haired and stooped,
white penny loafers on her feet.
She sleeps much of the time,
her hands softly crossed in her lap,
her face still and quiet.
What are her dreams now as she
heads to the land where no one is old —
or so it seems!
Or does she dream at all?
Do dreams disappear after a certain
time or do they transform
into memories
only?
I want to know that!
But I guess I will just have to wait
until I too put on
white penny loafers.

MOVING ON . . . OWEN

And so it goes . . .
Life moves on, and so do I —
and you — in very different
directions.
I guess I should be angry, or
upset, but I am not. You
didn't wait very long to find someone
else to love, but I so understand —
I could make you no promises
at all, much as I wanted to.
You gave me something I never had
before.
I opened up my heart to you and you
never once abused it —
you just allowed me
to be who I am and told me that I was
okay.
That in itself, was such an
extraordinary gift!
I wish that it all could be different.
I wish I could stay here but I
cannot.
Perhaps, as someone told me, you
are training wheels for the
real thing.
If that is so, he will be very, very
wonderful indeed!
If not, well that is life,
isn't it?

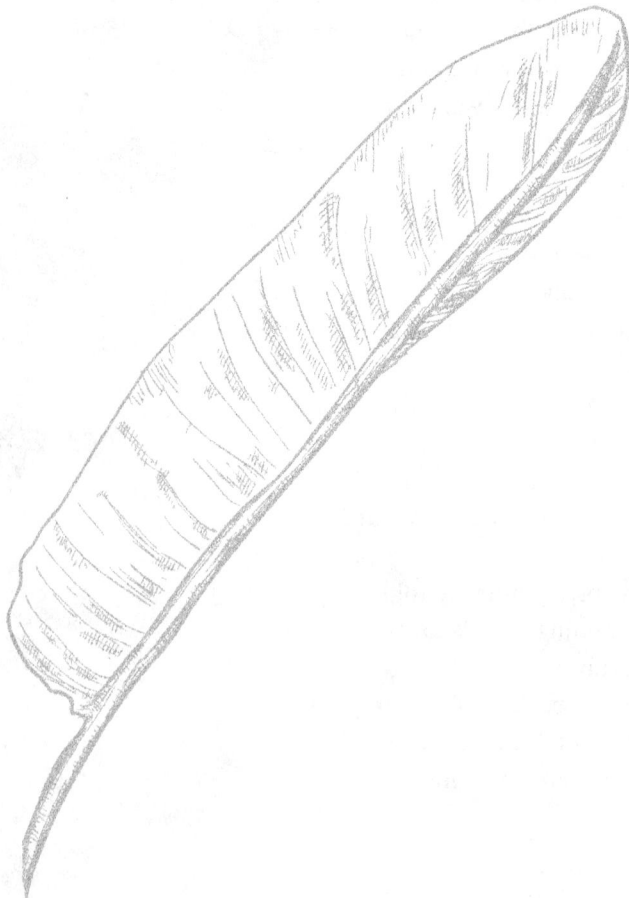

THE CALL

I got a phone call from Owen, the man
I wrote about in **Moving On** —
telling me
that *she*
was Not the One
after all.
Three dates, the last one
a disaster.
What is it with guys that they cannot
wait until the body is *cold*
before they search out another one???
Couldn't he have waited just a
few more weeks until
I left???
So part of me, the part I am not
totally proud of,
felt totally gleeful that I could
NOT be so easily replaced.
And I know that!!!
The other part felt such incredible compassion.
I know so well the depth of loneliness,
when there is no one there to
hold and to
love,
when we know that is what we are
made to do.
I will see him again, and God
only knows what will happen
then.
But I see for sure that this is not
The End.

can i?

I am totally awash
in tears.
They flow inside of me —
and outside.
At times I
cannot breathe because they
flood every part of
who I am.
Am I crazy to be leaving this Place
Where I was truly Born?
Am I crazy to be going back to
where everything and
everyone is private, where
the biggest hello is walking
to and from the car — if one is lucky?
I have moved from
conservative matron, member of
the tennis club, neckties and pantyhose,
country club dances and horse shows,
to swimming in
pools free from any restriction, including
clothes.
I am *NOT* a swinger, but what I know
for sure is that there is freedom out there —
in all that I have learned, in all that I believe,
and in all that I have become.
I have pushed aside so many of my barriers,
and the depth of who I am has become alive with
smiles and laughter.
Not the tears that drench me now.

Can I do this? Can I continue to be the
person I have become —
back there?
Can I?
I do not know.
Time will tell.

FEEL GOOD

Walking up the street this morning
I passed a little boutique
that had bars of soap
for sale — Feel Good the name.
I thought about buying the soap
but then memories of feeling good —
of pleasure in touching the body —
came back and I saw the visions of
no, no, coming into
my head, as sometimes my thoughts
do.
What nonsense, my Self thought.
Cleansing the body was always
an essential part of life for sure, but to
have the sheer pleasure of luxuriating
in lovely suds and awesome
fragrance was considered
frivolous, extravagant,
even sinful, if you get my meaning,
and could lead you
down the road
to Who Knows Where . . .
I finished my errands and
again walked by the little boutique
that had bars of soap
for sale — Feel Good the name.

And since you know me so
well, I expect you know
what I did.
Now the water is drawn,
my clothes are no where
to be found,
and I am touching, with pleasure,
all parts of my body,
fragrant and clean and
oh, so fine!

BLACK IN — OR OUT . . .

Living in southern California, I
have always wondered why
women wear black.
Black pants, black sweaters, black
shoes, black coats — well, you
get the idea.

In this gorgeous, glorious, color-filled,
   environment, is it that they don't want
to compete with all the colors of all the
                              flowers,
            knowing they don't
stand much of a chance in
         this realm of radiance?

            Or is it that
         they don't have to think
      about what matches what, or
      doesn't — which makes life
            very easy?
   Or is it because black covers cellulite
and bouncing bulges better than any other
         color ever created?

               Or maybe it is that black hides
               a multitude of spills and
               stains, not a very glamorous
               way to end a poem
               but perhaps that is the real
               truth!

MASTURBATION

We talk on the phone.
You talk about the places
on my body
that haven't been
touched
in a long, long time.
I feel the warmth move slowly
...there...
...where...
warmth is often slow to come
now.
By the time you hang up
I am hung up and
...ready...
So...
I take Matters into
my own hands.
And at that most special moment
the cat jumps on my back!
That ends THAT!
Then, moving once more
as women will do
the rhythm
...grows...
...grows...
and then...and then...
...again...and
...again...
I lay back, satisfied at least
until you are
...There.

THE OLD STORY . . .

Let go of the story! Tear it up into
little pieces!
Light a fire and burn the fucking thing!
Flush it down
the toilet!
And flush it again — just to be sure!
You can go over all the years — or
seconds, or minutes or hours or
months of
pain and turmoil and
what mother did — or did not do
or what dad did — or did not do
or all the what if's and if only's and
WHATEVER!!!
and tell me,
just tell me,
how does that serve you???
How does your knowing add
one bit of joy, or happiness,
to your life?
Let *go* of the story!
Forgive yourself for all
you believe you did —
or
did not do.
Forgive others for all
you believe they did —
or
did not do.

For, really, the only answer to it all is
Forgiveness,
and from the moment
that is done, from that very most precious
moment
your light will shine, God's
light will shine
and you will know *for sure*
that all that you are
is absolutely perfect
and how you were
absolutely meant to be!

JUDGMENTS

Today it was pointed out, in a
most loving and gentle way,
how judgmental I am.
And I saw for certain the truth
told to me in that moment.
Here I am, preening peacock of self-righteous
self-importance, looking at all those
who I judge
have not
done their work, and thinking how
far above them I am
because of the work *I* have done!
And I had to admit that indeed
I have been absolutely gloating in my own
self-importance.
My life is my life, and I did not exactly
jump to the Higher View myself.
But I think I am making some steps now, or
at least I am willing to not
stay
where I was.
Today I acknowledge that I choose to give
each person the dignity of finding their
own way,
in their own time,
through their own process,
however long it takes.
And if I can help,
I will.

I forgive myself for all the judgments
I have made,
and I pray God to give me
the humility and the kindness I so need
to allow others
to walk their path
as they will.

SATURDAY AT THE FARMER'S MARKET

It started out cloudy this morning,
but lasted only a nanosecond.
I walked to the Market in a heavenly daze
of soft sunshine and delicate ocean breezes
whispering to me from the west.
Only two more times to visit this
most extraordinary place before I move away,
and I gather in my arms
bunches of sunflowers and lavender and
bags of peaches and grapes, tomatoes and salad
fixings scattered with salad flowers,
yellow and white.
I am still amazed — after all this time —
that I have been blessed to live in
all this richness — and how grateful
I am that I could embrace it
throughout the changing seasons.
Had I the nerve, I would prostrate myself
before these gods of plenty here on Arizona Street
and thank them for
everything they have provided for me
during my stay.
But instead I enjoy a luscious sample
of the newest plums,
letting the juice dribble
down my chin in total and complete
satisfaction!

DINNER

He has just left. I have cleaned up after
the dinner he prepared (which was awesome,
I might add) —
and I am feeling complete
and filled. We shopped together, buying all
the ingredients, prowling up and down
the aisles for things we needed —
and didn't need, and stopping
to kiss and touch when we felt like it.
How wonderful! And there were other things
to do when we got back to my apartment, so
it was at least three hours before we even thought
about what dinner would be like.
The appetizer was just outstanding, however!
After dinner, we sat and held each
other, quietly being. Seldom in our lives anymore do
we get to just be.
We talked of my leaving and he could now
ask questions, unlike before.
He said, the road to your future lies on
the east coast, and you must go back.
It was very huge for him to say that.
It is true, and I am not sure what it will mean
for me — or for him.
Time will handle that.
And as we sat looking into
each other's eyes, I saw
something far different from what
I have ever seen before.
Quietly and gently, he let me go deep within
to the very depths of
his soul and let me
rest there.

How true it is that, when we cut through all the
layers of who we say we are,
when all of it
is pushed out of the way,
we see, and let others see in us,
the absolute, authentic Self.
I wrapped myself in the
Magnificence of that golden, glorious moment
and smiled at God. And for sure
He smiled back at me.

THE GUEST ROOM

Monday, September 6 — a week before
the movers come to pack
me up and take me away.
It will be a hot one today, but
the early morning is bright and beautiful
and gentle breezes rattle my
verticals, telling me life
is very gorgeous out there!
I have started the packing and
box after box after box fills what was
the guest room. So I shut
that door.
The rest of my apartment looks yet
just the same.
This has been a lovely place
to live and, yes, to love — but also
a haven for that deeply solitary part of me
I cherish so deeply.
Two years have quickly passed,
and there is barely
a day I haven't loved being here.
I walk into the kitchen, generally a
place where heavenly fragrances tease
the nose and gorgeous meals taunt
the palate — I have created little of that.
Dining for one does not excite me much,
and the various dietary needs of
my friends
make dining out
the easy way!
The living/dining rooms have been a
constant source of comfort. The fireplace
has warmed me, albeit not much, but the cozy
blanket snuggled me and warmed me
when the fire did not.

The bedroom — so large and airy and bright —
has been a lovely source of rest — and energetic
relaxation — no complaints
about this room for sure!
But it is in the guest room where
I have spent the most time because
the computer is there.
Enormous nemesis, the battles between us
are bitter and endless, but it is here
I have drawn the deepest comfort
and joy as I write out
my heart
in words I never knew I had.
 I will leave the computer running until the very end.
My heart needs to know it has a safe place
to spill over and
flow.
I go out on the balcony, taking
the ever-present cup of coffee with me.
Here I first noticed the
bottle brush tree and hummingbirds —
here the first poem I wrote was born.
My flowers, now bedraggled and forlorn,
will guard the edge the next few days
so Amos won't nosedive over.
He did that once, his explorations
too rambunctious, landing
three stories down with nothing worse
than a cut lip and the idea that
height is better thought about
than explored.

I will miss my little apartment, perhaps more
than I realize, but I have my house to
go back to, and spaciousness and light
and air and a
different kind of comfort, for sure.
It is home, there is family,
and I will have another
room where my heart
can open up
and my computer battles
continue.
I open another box in the guest room
and start to pack more of my life
away — to reopen it again
in a few weeks.

WISDOM

I have started saying my goodbyes to friends —
all of whom have made such
an incredible difference in my life.
Younger than I, their energy
and enthusiasm for living has so
added to *my* energy and enthusiasm.
And I totally forget
that oft times they are young enough
to be my daughters.
I wish I could give back to
them some of my own aging wisdom
but there seems to be
so little.
But I have it inside —
somewhere.
If they find anything to value in the
years I have lived,
perhaps it is this.
I have learned that
loving is ageless —
laughter is ageless —
hugging is ageless —
touching is ageless —
and all of this adds up to a
life well lived, and more than that,
fully lived — even though it
has taken me so many years
to get that.
But they are learning how
to do it **now**, joyfully and with no
expectations.
How extraordinary their lives
will be
when they reach my age!

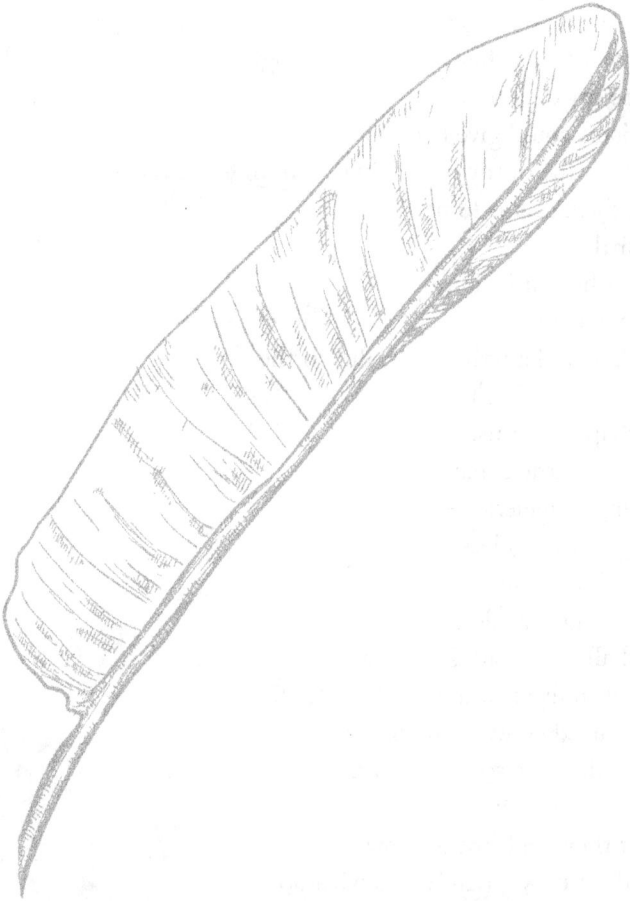

FIRST CLASS

Amos scratches at the packed boxes,
almost as if, like the kitty litter he uses,
he can cover up what doesn't smell good
and it will all go away.
He's not too keen on this move, and
he looks at me as if I have
taken total leave of
my senses for disrupting our lovely routine.
And that, of course, leads me to
Question my
Own Sanity! (I am so influenced by
my cat!)
As if to mock my decision making process,
the west coast insists on being totally sparkling,
alive with sunshine and teasing breezes,
while the east coast is waterlogged by the remains
of the huge hurricane — water, water
everywhere.
What am I — Crazy? Mad? *Loco*? (Note how
I throw a bit of *espanol* into my California life!)
I admit my craziness, and that is
all I have to say except —
the heart knows what it must do, and
it is doing it.
And Amos is coming along for the ride —
like it or not —
First Class!

BEVERLY HILLS THERAPIST

Tomorrow I make my last trip,
at least in this chapter of my Adventure,
to Beverly Hills. Can you imagine
me — *moi*! — in Beverly Hills?? I'll drive down
Charleville — better than Wilshire or the
freeways — too much traffic —
although Charleville takes longer.
A lovely ride down shaded streets that shows me
how the other half lives. Not the
très très élégant side of Beverly Hills — but
exclusive enough (one cross street is Rodeo Dr.)
and I feel pretty *élégant* myself
driving there.
I'll have coffee at this chic little coffee shop I love and then go
to say goodbye to my therapist. That will be
very sad for me. Of Swedish heritage, raised
Lutheran, as was I, she understands me —
and my background —
as if she were my twin.
This gorgeous woman, with the spiky gray hair, is really tough,
but beautifully gentle as well, and
calls me on **all** my stuff con-tin-u-ous-ly!
I have laughed hysterically with her — shared
many of my foibles and peccadilloes,
perceived sins and failures —
have learned that taking everything
so seriously has kept me totally out of being
my Authentic Self — who I really, truly am.
I will so miss her laughter and humor and
her extraordinary brilliance with
therapeutic technique.
She has taught me so much!

I will stay in touch as I want to know
her next steps in life and I will want
to share mine and
to hear her say,
when I get weird in my head,
Turn down K-FUCK radio, would you please? —or —
Give the Shitty Committee that resides
in your head
a break — send them on a very long
vacation —permanently!!
I will remember those statements with humor,
and her with such love.
Thank you so very, very much.
I'll talk to you soon again, Arlene!

SEPTEMBER

Even in California, in September,
the leaves change color
and drop.
I don't know why that surprises
me so,
but it does.
They fall easily now,
browned and dry from
lack of rain,
sunburned from the
everlasting California
sunshine.
I expected it to be green
here — forever.
Almost like I expected
to live here — forever.
But no longer.
I crave the fullness of life
I have seen here,
green and fresh and filled
with the glowing radiance of
youth. But more and more often
the mirror is telling me that
what radiance I have left
belongs someplace else
where it still can shine.
My leaves indeed are changing color
but are not quite ready
to drop.
And perhaps my own rich autumn hues,
such as they are,
can yet bring warmth
and brightness
somewhere else.

PENNSYLVANIA

OFF —

I have been off-computer, off-line,
and off-poetry for many days now,
and on to unpacking the boxes
that followed me cross country,
as easy a move as easy can be.
The last of the jammed bags
of packing paper go out tonight,
and the last
of the broken down boxes
out — to wherever tons of paper and boxes
rest in peace.
Was I ever away?
Was I ever living a life in
California?
How do I define myself — or
rather — redefine myself
in this new life?
I have no knowledge — yet — of
how that will be,
but I do know that if love provides
the answers,
I will be just fine.

COLD — AND WARMTH

It got cold last night —
cold enough so that when I get up
to pee, my feet on the tiles feel
like I am walking on 6 x 6 inch ice cubes.
And it is only early October!
Amos doesn't like it much either and
as I crawl back under the warm
comfort of covers, I feel a furry
lump where he sneaked in, now warmed up by
where I had just been and in no way
eager to move!
We battle for the space and you know
who won!
Awake now at early dawn,
the steaming coffee warms my cold hands
and opens my heart.
Amos jumps into my lap and
as he settles in while I
read the paper
it is his turn to bring warmth to me.
We sit that way a long time,
and as the house grows warm,
we let go of each other —
me to start my day — he
to chase his toy mice and then
to find a
sunny spot to nap.
Cold — and warmth — work well together!

ASCENSION

Early morning.
The sun begins its newest ascension and
as I watch it move amidst the trees
behind my house,
golden leaves turn luminescent,
shimmering with radiance for
a few more days while
on their way to
eternal rest.
Isn't that the way of life?
Like the now golden leaves,
we too can show the radiance
that has been ours from
the very beginning,
Laying to rest the fears and guilt
that have burdened us
forever, we glow in the Sunlight
sparkling and glistening
for all to see!

Had we only known this earlier!

PRAYER SHAWL

Take this, my friend Sandy said, putting
two large balls of yarn and knitting needles
in my lap.
Knitting is very good for a subluxated
finger, you know.
The dim, dark shadows of
forgotten stitches
slowly clear as I cast on.
And fingers,
unused to such activity,
begin to move again
in the creation process.
This will be a prayer shawl, she said,
sent to warm a child in Russia
who lived through the horrible nightmare
of murder and terrorism.
Many hands work together
knitting love and prayers of healing
into the soft warmth
soon to enfold these little ones
so deeply in need.
Mine is almost finished now,
many miscast stitches,
not at all perfect, and I am somewhat
embarrassed by this.
But I will send it anyhow — all the prayers
and love I have to give are present here.
And that is where the healing is.

THE STORM

October turned the other cheek this week.
The glorious golden days
turned to muck and drizzle
and rain, and heavy winds
sent branches brushing at my bedroom
window, begging to come in to the
warmth of my midnight bed.
I heard. And I was afraid.

I lay there then as the saturated dawn
began to wring itself out,
putting aside its tears for the moment
and bravely allowing itself the
slightest smile. But the darkness
came back, and the winds and
heavy rain and brushing branches
tried once again to
enter in my bedroom window,
begging to come in to the
warmth of my morning bed.
I heard. And I was afraid.

What if this were to last
forever, I thought. What if I cannot
brave the storms or
stand the cold that follows the
glorious golden October days.
My heart then began the transformation,
warming my soul with the
love only the heart can give.

And, opening the window wide,
I embraced the winds of fear
and the cold of days
growing short.
At that very moment
the heavy rain became as
teardrops on my cheeks.
And the branches sent forth soft leaves
to caress my pain-wracked body.

As the sun broke through the clouds
in magnificent radiance,
acceptance slipped into
the warmth of my daylight bed,
Afraid no longer,
I slept.

MY BUDDHA

He stands there, hands outstretched
over his head, a huge
smile on his face,
and a wonderful tummy just
made for rubbing.
And there are those who ask
why in heaven's name I would
have something like *that* in
my house.
A few years ago, I wouldn't have
but it is different now.
I can and want to relate to joy and
laughter.
I am tired of pain and guilt and
suffering.
And to rub my Buddha's tummy
just makes me feel really good.
And who knows? Maybe him too!
Perhaps there is something to the
Jesus I have learned about all
my life.
And perhaps one day I will return to
that image that now just makes me
tired and sad.
Perhaps one day the Buddha's
path could lead me right to the feet of
the Christ.
And what I want to see are his hands
outstretched over his head and
a huge smile on his face.
Tummy not necessary!
Just a joy-filled love of God
He shows the world.
Couldn't that
change everything??

LAMENTATIONS — ELECTION DAY (NOVEMBER)

Awakened before the dawn of dawn
I hear the wind, her voice racing through
my window screen, lamentations loud and wild
and filled with sadness,
never ending.
And it is deeply dark.
It is then I know for sure —
as sure as if I had stayed up to watch it all
unfold
as pundits and talking heads did what they do best . . .
talk.
How is it that they who are *right*
do not see the horrible danger
we are in.
Who will our country turn on next?
Who among us will be told they are less
than they are, entitled to nothing because
they are . . .
different.
Who among our women will find herself
in deepest darkness, covered in blood
because a *right* man gave her
no choice.
Who will be the next victim
where our young and mostly poor
will give their own blood
killing others who are
different . . .
because those who are *right*
have said this is what must be done.
Who will stand in fields no longer gold —
where once the wild things lived —
now black with sludge
and profit
for those, mostly *right*,
who will take —
and run.

I see this as a very dark time
and all I have to give, and must give, is
love.
Because that can be the turning point
and it is all I have.
But first I must put out the fires of my own
anger and fear and know
that the dark times will come
and the dark times will go.
And Spirit will give us all that we need
when it is time.

THE SCREAM

I took a ride in the country today.
Or what used to be country before I
went away. Tall bare trees waved to me
as I drove past, but the fields
of wheat
of corn
of swaying grass
have been replaced
by architectural blights and
designer landscapes, where once
the countryside lay . . .
open and free.
Four car garages speak of
more than enough
horsepower
and gated entrances tell me that
not all are welcome here
anymore.
What does the land say when the red stakes
are driven into her soul . . .
when 'dozers rip open her fertile body, wet cement
replacing the life giving seeds planted there
for generations.
And the little creatures —how do they deal? Their homes
now gone, their lives shattered
by bricks
and boards
and heavy stone driveways.
I saw one tonight, a gentle possum by the side of the road,
blood running
from its wide opened mouth
in the silent scream we choose not
to hear any longer.
And I drove by.
There was nothing I could do.
And I wept.

SATURDAY MORNING

Working in the kitchen this morning
preparing for a dinner party I thought
I must call Mom.
I haven't thought that in so long.
Perhaps it was the fragrances from the stove
or even the thought of approaching Thanksgiving
but there it was — I must call Mom.
We didn't talk much, she and I, and certainly
never about
Anything Important.
She had lost contact with her Self
so long ago and whatever was hidden within
had been covered with layers of insecurities
and shame, relieved only by the occasional
bouts of drinking, often sneaking directly from
the bottle and replacing it with water so Dad
never saw.
She taught me that, but I did her one better,
adding food coloring so nothing ever looked
watered down.
The kitchen was not where she excelled.
If it wasn't perfect she was a failure
once again, some unknown Voice telling
her so.

I have picked up some of that but have let
it go, almost, so that I can have joy in the
company of others.
And that was what I wanted to share with her —
that although the winter stew was sending forth
the most delicious aromas, the butcher had
let me down — the meat was tougher than tough
even though he had promised me
otherwise.
Can't do much about that now!
So I will hope for the best
enjoy my guests
and send forth a prayer of thanksgiving
for my friends and all the blessings of my life
and of course
for the butcher!

GREEN EYES

I'm at that stage in life when
little arms flung
'round my neck mean more than
just about anything in the world.
And so it happened. A tiny
whirlwind, blond hair swirled high
above her head and held in place
with a red rubber band, raced towards me,
arms outstretched, leaping into·
my arms with a hug that only a
beloved grandchild
can give.
Months ago I last saw her — but now a
big girl, almost three.
I held her back so that I could look at
this joy filled child so excited to
see me.
She stopped then, staring at me with
a look of such wonder.
Grans — that's what she calls me — Grans, she said,
your eyes are so green!! And she hugged me hard
again.
My green eyes filled with mist, for what
first she saw were the windows to my soul.
I will never know if she saw anything else,
but I hope and pray that she will always
know that what fills my green eyes is
love beyond measure for this
little whirlwind, her blond hair swirled high
above her head and held in place
with a red rubber band.

THE THREE YEAR OLD

Today I woke up as a
human being, the divine part
definitely **not there.**
It has been
a long while since I have
felt this way and it is NOT
a good feeling at all!!!
Work is not happening,
relationships that feed my
soul seem to have been blown away
by the chill winds of November
and I feel alone and bereft.
I am like a cranky three year old
(and having just been with one
I recognize the signs),
who doesn't know what
she wants or how to get it.
But unlike the three year old who
throws a tantrum, I withdraw
and hide.
This grown up child wants so badly
to crawl up into the lap of
consolation and love and be held
until the confusion and fear fall away
and life feels right again.
I don't know where to go for that here —
for that touch and assurance
that will allow my petulant, pouty child
to slide off the lap knowing that tomorrow
it will all be
okay.

Sometimes, I guess, one must be the parent to
one's Self, to sit with her and tell her that
all
is just fine and
she is too
just as she is, all
cranky and needy.
And to remember that
tomorrow is, after all,
another day.

SNOWFALL

Clouds have rumbled in
after days of lovely sun and
December breezes that put a perfect,
diamond-like chill in the air.
A snowflake falls, and then another
and then more, and little ones race outdoors,
giggling, jumping, tumbling,
tongues out to catch each perfect
flake and taste every imagined delectable
snowflake flavor —
as only children can.
And as the flakes fall
and cover the ground, little
snow angels abound — evidence for sure
that
tiny celestial beings are
in our midst.
Young couples come out, scarved and mittened,
to clear a path and throw snowballs at each other,
laughing with love as the soft snow
covers hair and lashes and eyes filled with mischief
that only lovers
understand.
I put on my jacket and go outside, to feel the snow
as it lands softly on my face and my shoulders, each
flake telling a story of creation unlike any other.
I stand a long time, unable to move, as the flakes
cover me, and I know that I will stand there until
I am no more.
My body is cold and my spirit asks only to become
part of a greater love than exists for me here.
If I am remembered for having tried,
for having given even a little to better my world,
then I will have accomplished
Something — maybe Everything.
Silent the streets are now.

As the snow blankets me in its gentleness and purity
I know that life is such a wondrous gift.
Sinking into the beauty of total
Whiteness, I feel my Soul move out
into the Universe and I am
nothing — yet Everything —
once again.

RED FOX

While backing out of my friend Pat's driveway
I stopped to let the traffic pass
and something else came into view —
the Red Fox.
Intent on his purpose,
eyes straight ahead,
dirty, disheveled and wet
as December rain
he crossed the road
right in front of me and
into the bushes
before I
lost sight of him.
What does a Red Fox do
in the midst of Suburbia, I wondered.
Obviously he could care less
about my wonderment
and as he emerged from the brush
my red-coated friend took off
like red lightening around the corner
of the house.
Good luck Mr. Fox I said.
I don't know what you are after
but may whatever it is have
good luck as well!
And I drove away.

MAMA SCHULZ

I am writing Christmas cards today,
many memories of many friends
over many decades.
But one special one
stands out unlike any other —
Mama Schulz.
How I wish I could tell her and that she could
understand
how much she has meant to me.
She sits there, tiny, fragile, beautiful
as always, the lights of her life
dimmed —
no memories of even
yesterday.
Ninety-six years old now and for ninety of
those, she gave us all
such wisdom and joy and
so much love.
Is there even a tiny connection to that time
when, visiting with the kids,
we would wake up to Florida
grapefruit cut, a maraschino cherry
in each center, the start of a breakfast
unlike any other
anywhere!
Hours by the pool
or at the ocean,
waves of Atlantic seawaters
knocking us down!
And laughter, always laughter.
Wonderful dinners and long walks
in the neighborhood after dark,
gazing at the stars and moon
of a warm, southern sky.

And always Mama Schulz waiting for us,
willing to listen to, and comment on (for sure!)
our Adventures!
Brilliant, compassionate, strong in
her faith and in her Russian heritage,
I remember her only as
she was those years ago.
I love you, Mama Schulz!
Thank you for all you have given to me and
to our family.
As you wait to go Home
know you will be the Angel among angels.
And one day,
I will see you again.

WOODSTREAM DRIVE

I open the door and walk into
my house.
Therein lies all that I have and all that
I love
except, perhaps, the kitchen floor —
a reminder of decades past
when yellow linoleum
was In.
Each room created after my divorce, a desire
to bring all the love that had been dead for years
transformed into colors and joy and comfort
for me — and all others
who might share it with me.
But that didn't happen here.
A house is not a home, someone said.
And now I know that for sure.
I cannot put my arms around it nor
hold it tight to my breast and kiss the
face and hair of someone dear.
Or speak to it, or hear laughter or touch tears
unless they are my own.
As I walk silently from room to room I know
that I will leave this house.
I want to find home before it is
too late.
I had hoped I could live here again
but I know I cannot.
So I will return to sunshine and
friendships and places where I am
welcomed and have a sense of purpose.
And, for now anyhow, to a small apartment —
filled with colors, joy, and comfort
that I can, at last, call home.

LOVE

I am so in love!
With whom? you ask.
I pause. I don't know —
and does it really matter?
Must one be in love with
some *one* or can one
just be in love?
If I put a limit on my loving,
I limit my self.
But if I open my self up
to all of the world,
if I love it all,
what gifts I receive!
And they receive mine.
How very rich then we all are!

SNOWSTORM IN SUBURBIA

It is nearly the end of January —
but still not near enough.
I awaken to the grayness of a
Saturday morning, and then remember —
it's Snowstorm in Suburbia day!
I have been away just long enough to feel
my heart pick up speed
and sense the excitement of
Something Highly Unusual about
to happen.
Around 10:00 the first flakes fall,
floating lazily through the still
morning.
By 10:30 they mean business,
dressing my yard in the virginal
whiteness of a bride awaiting. And the trees
become the groom, strong and solid
and quietly adorned.
By 1:00 I can't see much of
anything at all, and all
the TV weather prognosticators are
deliriously comparing this storm
to one back in the 50's or 70's —
but then again it could just be bigger
than any other.
The roads are pretty quiet,
except for an occasional SUV.
One moves too quickly
under the testosterone power
of its driver — and then
skids into a tree down the street.
A friend phones me from the
airport — just to say adios as he
jets off to Cancun — if he can
get off to Cancun.

Owen calls to remind me that it
is 83 degrees and sunny
in Santa Monica
and that tomorrow he will go
biking by the ocean.
Lighting a fire in my fireplace
I wrap myself in its warmth
and sip a cup of tea.
And I know for sure that when
January comes again and
the snow begins to fall
I will call my friends
in warmer climes —
just to check in!

EPILOGUE

MY KIDS ARE NOW 48...
   (they are twins)

You must publish your poetry,
my friends said.
What?
I said.
It's wonderful, the words are brilliant,
the ideas . . . well, some are a bit
X-rated, but others . . .
Not good enough,
I said.
Just words, thoughts, ideas pouring forth
when I need them to.
Nothing more.
And besides, what would my kids say?

+   +   +   +

Today, a decade-plus later, here I am
publishing my poetry!
Happy, confident, strong, alive,
creative.
Ready to let people in, to see ME –
and maybe even to like my words.
Besides, my kids are now 48!

+   +   +   +

Daydreams come . . .
Oprah has me on her show, sitting in her garden,
while she interviews me!
And . . . OMG! The Today Show!   And Stephen Colbert!
One night, while fixing dinner,
the phone rings!
It's OSLO!!!!!
So, if Bob Dylan can win a Nobel prize, then

Why Can't I?!?!?
Oh my!

+   +   +   +

. . . Back to Reality.
Life — and dreams — keep moving me on —
as do yours, I am sure.
Wherever they lead you, just remember
one thing . . .
Your kids are now 48!

ABOUT THE AUTHOR

Karen Schulz is originally from Minnesota, but has lived most of her life on the East Coast except for a time in southern California. When she is not writing poetry, she spends her time gardening, watercolor painting, hiking, and not-very-good bowling! She lives in suburban Philadelphia with her rescue cat, Artemis.

Contact Karen at PoetGardenerKaren@gmail.com